Manners & Etiquette @ Work Place

Seema Gupta

V&S PUBLISHERS

Published by:

F-2/16, Ansari Road, Daryaganj, New Delhi-110002
☏ 011-23240026, 011-23240027 • *Fax:* 011-23240028
Email: info@vspublishers.com • *Website:* www.vspublishers.com

Regional Office : Hyderabad
5-1-707/1, Brij Bhawan (Beside Central Bank of India Lane)
Bank Street, Koti, Hyderabad - 500 095
☏ 040-24737290
E-mail: vspublishershyd@gmail.com

Branch Office : Mumbai
Jaywant Industrial Estate, 2nd Floor–222, Tardeo Road
Opposite Sobo Central Mall, Mumbai – 400 034
☏ 022-23510736
E-mail: vspublishersmum@gmail.com

Follow us on:

All books available at **www.vspublishers.com**

© Copyright: V&S PUBLISHERS
Edition 2017

The Copyright of this book, as well as all matter contained herein (including illustrations) rests with the Publisher. No person shall copy the name of the book, its title design, matter and illustrations in any form and in any language, totally or partially or in any form. Anybody doing so shall face legal action and will be responsible for damages.

PUBLISHER'S NOTE

In line with a number of books on *Personality Development*, V & S Publishers have come out with the revised edition of the book, **Manners & Etiquette @ Work Place** written by the well-known author, psychotherapist and counsellor, Seema Gupta. The book is a complete guide on the Right Manners and Etiquette that a person should practise to develop a good behaviour and a pleasing personality. What should be his dress code and posture, his language, his way of greeting people, his conduct while working with his colleagues in office or at home, telephone manners, written communication, etc., all these and many more have been elaborately discussed and explained by the author.

This book is meant for readers of all ages, particularly for youngsters, for a well-mannered person is always welcome and liked by everyone in a society. By reading this book, one can learn the acumen of polished behaviour and groom oneself accordingly to outshine in all spheres of life. Good mannerisms and etiquette can impress people instantly and you can be a winner in whichever circumstance or field you are in. Hence, this book is a must for all those who aim to make it big in their lives and win everyone's heart!

INTRODUCTION

Manners & Etiquette @ Work Place are not always present in most people. Keeping a professional atmosphere in the workplace is a very important part of keeping the company admirable and respectable in the eyes of both its customers and its employees.

Behaving in the workplace with courteous and respect is an essential part of growing professionally and becoming a more mature person in the corporate world. To ensure proper etiquette, office manners must be observed at all times. There are a lot of ways to observe proper etiquette in the workplace and most of these conducts were already introduced to us while we were still young. Still some of the things always need a reminder.

The posture of a person needs to be very appealing that would attract other person immediately. While sitting and standing, you need to be attractive enough to have a good posture. Also impatience is the enemy of good posture.

Dress code should be according to the occasion. Good taste and simplicity of clothes is the key feature with the element of proper colours, fitting, great hold on accessories will lead to the appropriate dressing for the event.

The behaviour needs to be good enough to make right friends where one cultivate his/her charm.

A person should be able to introduce himself, whether it is a business introduction or maybe in the family. Introducing ourselves to the public is the most important thing a person needs to learn.

Extending greetings like shaking hands, saying nameste, dismissing or escorting someone is a good thing to learn and experience. It will help the people remember you for long.

Conversation is another necessary element where speaking skills, listening, conversational starters and avoiding slangs becomes a key feature to be taken good care of.

Telephone manner helps in getting the correct and sufficient information from the other party on line. Like answering the phone, the timings, identification, returning calls, messages, wrong number and the correct way to end the phone conversation is very important.

While written communication is concerned, a person shouldn't take it as chore, instead he should practice the letter writing formula where the body and closure needs to be good and addressing the envelope is correctly done.

While hunting for a job, the resume, model biodata, application should be well informed and requires a special creativity which would impress the company to call you down for an interview session.

Finally etiquette at work is the most important phenomenon where you need to maintain the office code of behaviour, use the telephone tactics, handle the rivals, help other colleague, manage relations with the boss.

These key elements would help you in reaching at great heights (if applied carefully).

This following book would help you in knowing all the necessary things while applying for a job and keeping it for long in a good flow.

CONTENTS

1. Etiquette — The Keyword 9
2. Posture 11
3. Dress Code 15
4. Your Behaviour 22
5. Hi... Hello! 27
6. Extending Greetings 33
7. Conversation — Mind That Language 39
8. Telephone Manners..46
9. Written Communication..50
10. Job Hunting 58
11. Etiquette at Work 66

ETIQUETTE — THE KEYWORD

Lord Tredegar knew exactly how to handle a habit of several years. One of his servants reported this incident — "I remember the morning when Lord Tredegar was taken exceedingly ill. Instead of the usual nod of his head to me on my arrival, he said, 'Cronin, I think I'm dying'."

The years-old habit could not be amended in a moment. I knew that even Lord Tredegar in his more collected moments would not wish it so. So correctly I replied, 'Very good, my Lord', Thereafter, the normal silence between us was reestablished to our mutual satisfaction.

Etiquette and good manners are acquired through constant practice. They are inculcated from childhood and become habits by the time we grow up. Remember the times when you were irritated by your mother's constant nagging to clean up the mess in your room. But she was only trying to help you by merely cultivating the good habit of tidiness in you — such is the case with good manners.

Can the ability to get along with others be learnt or is it a trait that you are born with? While there are people who appear to be born charmers, most of us have to learn how to relate to others. Even the charmers often find that they have to refine their skills of communication. Do we all not envy that charming, selfconfident fellow who moves with grace? He has the ability to turn even the most embarrassing situations into playful witty moments by his intellect and good-natured humour. A person with a fine sense of etiquette exudes confidence. He is able to put everybody at ease, unmindful of their social rank or status.

Several years ago, John D. Rockfeller said, "The ability to get along with people is as purchaseable a commodity as sugar and coffee, and I pay more for that ability than any under the sun."

Good manners are essential in building good relationships with other people and they can ensure that you have a steady supply of support and cooperation.

The practice of etiquette can be traced back to the times of kings and emperors where the courtiers bowed before the royal family. The elders received due respect and youngsters never spoke harshly to their parents.

Over the centuries, considerable emphasis has been placed in various societies on the proper forms of behaviour. Across the globe, career diplomats, armed force personnels, business executives, and even politicians are put through stiff training where even the minutest of details in etiquette is not excused. Even in our social circle, have we not noticed that it is the persons with pleasing mannerisms who are the most popular? No doubt, they have an edge over others. Although in the informality that prevails today, interest in codified behaviour has declined, yet at our parties, wedding cremonies, funerals, deaths, seminars or business meetings, we do observe certain basic acceptable norms of human behaviour.

By cultivating correct mannerisms and using them constantly, we are sure to be able to tackle various social occasions with confidence. Our skills in the areas of courtesy, politeness and etiquette can never go wasted.

A senior British diplomat was on his way to a Diplomtic meeting in London when his young secretary began complaining about etiquette and diplomatic Bologna.

"Isn't it a lot of hot air?", asked the secretary. "All etiquette is hot air, my dear", answered the wise diplomat. "But that's what's in our automobile tyres and see how it eases the bumps."

POSTURE

It is bearing, disposition, demeanour and poise that determine the pattern of our lives. A man may stand erect or stoop, he may sit smartly or lazily, he may speak nicely and soothingly or crudely – these and their variations are all part of good manners. A good posture indicates your good upbringing and the poised human body is one that ought to look as nature meant it to do so – upright, straight and beautiful. It is in the poised and healthy body that the poised and healthy mind is most often found.

Sitting Pretty

Anyone and everyone always sits down but graceful sitting begins with the manner in which you approach your chair. The first thing to bear in mind is that the act of sitting down should be done quietly. You should not plonk yourself down on a chair or scramble for a seat. Deliberate controlled movements are needed.

Hands: While sitting down, hands are particularly important. It is your hands that pose a problem, if you do not know what to do with them. Your nervousness may be apparent from the tremor through your hands. You should therefore learn how to place your hands properly either on the hands of the chair, or on your lap, or else they will get in your way and look very ungainly. Hands that are relaxed give you an aura of serenity and poise. Avoid jerky movements.

Legs: Legs also play an important role in your self-composure, poise and confidence. Do not shake or jerk your legs constantly. Besides being an unwelcome distraction to others, they look indecent. The cardinal rule for a lady when she sits is to keep her knees together.

Talking while sitting: When carrying on a conversation while sitting, you should be careful that your body movements are well synchronized so that they project a good personality. These movements become an aid to your posture. Smiles, acknowledgements, nods and so on should be combined with all these.

Standing

Standing is sometimes more difficult than sitting. One reason is that it causes more strain. There are various modes of standing —

(a) Standing straight with your hands hanging loosely at the sides.

(b) With your feet a little apart and your hands clasped behind you — this is termed standing at ease.

(c) Slight stooping or bowing as a mark of respect.

(d) Some people prefer standing with their hands on their hips. This is the worst form of standing and indicates that the person has no manners at all. It not only shows disrespect to others but also portrays an indifferent aggressive attitude.

(e) If you are dealing with a V.I.P., it would be better to adopt a posture of alertness instead of one of laid-back serenity.

Talking while standing: When you are holding a conversation with another person and both are standing, your attention should not be diverted. But if you are sitting when another person strikes up a conversation, you should get up immediately and talk to him. You should not let your attention be diverted elsewhere. The only

exception to the rule is if you are the host and have the responsibility of welcoming and seeing to the convenience of your guests, it is permissible for you to allow your attention to wander while in conversation.

Good Posture Habits

By teaching your child good posture habits, you have not only saved his physique but a lot of future embarrassment as well.

Sitting with a straight back, standing with ease and walking with the head held high are the basics of a good posture.

Posture is very closely associated with one's nature. If you sit erect, use your hands properly and know how to manage your legs while sitting in a group, you portray an image of a confident and composed person. Fumbling with your things unnecessarily, shaking your legs, touching your nose, ears or hair, playing with your fingers — these give you away by demonstrating your nervousness. Correct your child whenever you find him stooping. Stop him firmly if he is getting into the habit of shaking his legs while in conversation. Teach him how to walk and sit gracefully. You can make him understand the importance of a good posture by showing him as two different persons with good and bad posture habits respectively. The difference is so obvious that it will not be difficult to explain the importance of good posture to him.

Impatience : Enemy of Good Posture

Have you ever noticed that person pacing up and down the floor, scratching his ear, poking his nose, cracking his fingers, or looking at his watch every 10 seconds? What did you say? "He is in a big hurry." For what? No Sir, he is only waiting for a table in this restaurant, for which the manager has already told him that it would take 10 minutes. He is just a very impatient man. And this is revealed in his posture habits. He forgets all the basics of good posture as this devil of a habit — impatience — takes over. So be warned, even if you are an impatient kind of person, hide it tactfully and maintain your poise and charm. Remember, a delay of a few minutes will not cause havoc in your life. The sky will still be there when you look up five minutes later.

Do's and Don'ts

Keep your back and head straight and don't stoop. Talk without shifting around in your chair. Sit with knees close together — never wide apart. Don't take up more space than required. Avoid making unnecessary and flamboyant gestures.

Don't sit too close to the persons on either side of you. If walking in a crowd, try keeping pace with others — don't lag behind or stride ahead. Don't stop suddenly — others will walk into you.

If walking with a lady, walk on the outer side somewhat protectively. Don't walk too fast so that she has to run to keep pace with you.

DRESS-CODE

(This chapter may be skipped by men as it focusses on the fairer sex.)

Dress to suit your figure, face and personality. Clothing — no matter how artfully designed, how perfectly made, how fashionably styled — must always be judged on the basis of its relationship to the wearer. When selecting clothes and accessories, you must have a complete understanding of yourself, your figure, face and personality — this will help you achieve distinction and personal attractiveness.

Costly the raiment as thy purse can afford,
Rich but not gaudy...
For apparel oft proclaims the man."
— Shakespeare

*G*ood taste may be defined as a refined look, leaning more towards the conservative and simple than a flamboyant spectacular look. Remember these points.

Avoid offensively revealing clothes. Never be ostentatious or over-ornamented. Avoid fancy jewelry for day-time wear. Do not follow fashion blindly. Make sure you are neat and clean.

Simplicity and Good Taste

Status symbols have never had more power than they have today. Titan watches, Action shoes, Big Joe's T-shirts, Kala Mandir sarees, City Look sweaters and Weekender shirts are taking over. But do not panic, if you cannot afford them. It is still possible to look good without investing so much in either your apparel or accessories. It is preferable to carry a good though small leather purse than to carry an ostentatious, flashy and more expensive one from Cottage Emporium.

A well-stitched reasonably priced *salwar* suit is much more appealing than a tightly fitting gaudy outfit from an expensive shop.

Natural fibres such as cotton, wool and silk are not only stylish but are also classic fibres that are acceptable in any place.

Select a good quality material and have it stitched by reliable tailor.

Flatter your figure and skin: A critical self-analysis is essential for you to get fully acquainted with your own body structure.

Slim figures: A slim, perfectly proportioned figure will have no problem with clothes. It is the overweight or too-thin that must be careful.

Plump figures: Those overweight should avoid horizontal lines, pleats, ribbing and tucking, contrasting colours, accentuating belts, yokes, etc. Instead they should go in for vertical lines, stripes, button front-closing from neck to hem.

Thin figures: The too-thin girl must wear garments that add to her figure giving an illusion of fullness.

Colours

As far as colours go, let us put them into the divisions give above.

Plump girls: Overweight girls/women should go in for staple colours of black, navy brown, or dark grey. Deep reds, darktoned greens, low-keyed purples also suit her. She should avoid shocking pink, fire-engine red, brilliant whites. The overweight should definitely avoid spotted prints, shiny finish and go in for small, patterned prints in muted colour combinations.

Thin girls: A thin girl on the other hand can wear staple colours but in heavier textures and contrasting lines that will seem to fill her out. A petite girl should never wear large or widely spaced prints.

Fitting In

Well-tailored clothes with appropriate curves and seams is the key to a good fit — not so tight that they wrinkle everywhere and not so loose that they hang. A *salwar* suit or a midi looks best when properly fitted. Most women have this misconception that they need only two or three blouses in basic colours to go with all their sarees. They also do not give much importance to the fitting of the blouse. An unmatched badly fitted blouse or an ankle-length petticoat mars the beauty of even the most expensive saree.

Colour Blending

Colour blending is a very important boost to one's personality. If you are fair, all colours will suit you, especially pastel colours such as pale pink, blue, lemon, beige, cream, light green etc. For a wheatish and dark complexion, slightly dark colours are used.

Colour combination is an important aspect of dressing. Most women go wrong by using one blouse (usually black) with all the sarees. If you can spend a bundle on a saree, why not make it look more presentable by investing one-tenth of its cost in accessories? Men too should be careful about their colour combinations. Oranges, pinks, yellows, reds and greens are considered ladies' colours. Men should avoid them. Their best colours are grey, beige, blue and attributes of their different hues.

Although age groups used to matter earlier, these days all colours are worn by people despite their age group. A few years back, it was believed that dull grey shades, all light colours and various shades of cream belonged to the older generation, whereas all bright colours were meant for young people. However, with changing times, these rules have undergone a tremendous change. Today, if you buy a pink saree with a navy blue border for your mother, she will not give it to your wife, saying it's not her age to wear such colours. Instead, she will wear it quite happily.

However, there is no denying that sober colours do belong to the upper age group (say, above 40), as they indicate their maturity and bright and gaudy colours and dresses adapt well with young ones and children who are full of youth and bubbling with energy. Thus, their brightness and freshness matches best with the bright colours. Children, however, can wear any colour. But their best bet is bright colours, since childhood represents freedom from all worries and troubles, a carefree attitude, and so do these colours.

Accessories

Purses: A purse is a major accessory for women and should be bought keeping in mind your requirements. A leather purse always looks better than that of foam leather. There are different purses for different occasions and purposes. If, for example, you have a baby and you need to carry his water bottle and a few other things in your bag, a clutch purse will not serve the purpose. It is better in such a case to buy a large leather bag, spacious enough to hold all these things. Keep the small beaded clutch purse for social evenings. A smart medium-sized bag with a shoulder strap should be kept for going to office.

Do not overload your bag. It is never considered good manners if you spend half an hour searching for your hanky scattering your belongings all over the place. A bulging bag is very inelegant.

Shoes: Buy shoes to go with your outfit rather than buying them at random and impulsively and then trying to make them match your clothes. If you cannot afford many pairs, shoes in the three basic colours of black, brown, and maroon will do. Though high heels are very fashionable, do not go in for them unless you are confident and comfortable in stillettos. If your toes are pinched and feet cramped in tight-fitting shoes, the agony will be reflected on your face, besides making you irritable and snappy. If you are uncomfortable with the height of your heels, you will be unduly concerned about maintaining your balance and normal gait.

Handkerchiefs: A hanky should always be part of a person's wardrobe. Delicate lace-edged handkerchiefs for women and full-sized white ones with thin stripes for men should be used. They should be spotless, neatly ironed and changed daily. Remember even a little thing like a hanky goes a long way in building your personality and image.

Jewellery: Avoid the tendency to bedeck yourself with loads of jewellery in an effort to show off what you have. For college students, small studs in the ears or small rings, or a single bangle are sufficient. If you don't want to wear gold, the market is full of chunky, inexpensive jewellery ideal for the college student. Keep the gold for weddings and other special occasions.

Match your jewellery with your outfit, keeping the occasion in mind. You cannot wear junk stuff with a Kanjeevaram saree to a wedding. If you are going for a formal party or a reception, a gold set (earrings, chain, bangles, ring – all with the same design) may be worn. Precious stones embedded in gold look elegant when worn with a saree of the same hue. Diamonds and pearls go with everything.

Grooming: Needless to say that a well-dressed person falls short of the mark if he/she has not paid attention to personal grooming. Deodorants/anti-perspirants are a must in our hot climate. Do not drench yourself in perfume or after-shave. Spray on just enough so that a pleasant smell emanates from you. You need not go in for imported perfumes. A dash of rose water in your bath will do the trick.

The indigenous *ittars* are as good as any imported perfume.

The Appropriate Dress

We dress for various occasions — attending office, a wedding, dance, party, or just an informal get-together with old friends. Clothes reflect the aspirations and psyche of the wearer. Just as a heavily embroidered saree on a picnic would be totally inappropriate, so would minis or jeans be frowned upon if worn by a girl when she meeets her prospective in-laws or husband-to-be for the first time. The same bright red outfit which looked stunning at a party will be a total misfit at a funeral. A nicely starched *kurta-pyjama* will look out of place at a business meeting where every other person present is dressed in a suit. Likewise, the same clothes you prefer to wear to office will not do for a formal garden party.

For example, you have recently got married and your husband is happy to escort you around in clothes of your own choice, be it jeans, skirts, etc. But it would be insensitive of you to wear the same clothes when he takes you to meet his old, conservative grandfather for the first time. A saree or even a modest *salwar-kameez* would be most suited in this instance. In the same way, your husband should not insist on wearing his cut-off jeans or shorts when your relatives come visting.

This reminds me of an instance. A friend of mine, soon after completing her MA, got a job as a lecturer in a college. She did not give much consideration to what she wore on her first day at college and ended up wearing the first available garment she found — a skirt. The moment she entered the gates, she was accosted by a group of seniors who on mistaking her for a fresher began ragging her. Her protests fell on deaf ears and they thought she was fooling them by saying she was a lecturer. Later, when the truth came out, she was the laughing stock of the whole campus.

Dresses for Children

Compared to their elders, children have a wider variety of clothes to choose from. While boys can wear a pant-shirt or *kurta-pyjama* combination for non-formal occasions, and a coat-pant, *shervani* or safari for formal affairs, girls can have their pick from a range of lovely frocks to suit every occasion. They can also wear a *lehanga-chunri* to weddings. Girls have the advantage over boys as they can even wear pants or shorts. When choosing clothes for children, keep in mind their convenience and comfort. A silk *shervani* for your son in May or a thin cotton dress for your daughter in December will not do. Avoid dressing very small babies and infants in expensive silks and too many frills or flounces.

YOUR BEHAVIOUR

'You're better than anyone else.
Forget about learning to be polite.
You don't need to be polite.
You have a divine right.
The 'Thank you' and 'You are welcome' brigade
are there to serve.
If you must say something
A couple of grunts should suffice.'

The day man left his abode in the jungle and proceeded to civilize himself and to lift himself to higher levels of achievement, was the point when social contacts began to have a special significance for him. Since then, he started judging himself and continues to strive for the betterment of his personality.

Your personality sets you apart from the rest of the crowd. It manifests itself in your taste, fine sense of aesthetics and your way of dealing with others. The basis for a good personality is a good behaviour pattern: how good you are at making friends, how you handle your rivals, your class and style, how you conduct yourself at public places and your inherent charm, decorum and dignity which can quietly affirm your good upbringing and background.

Making Right Friends

When life was simpler, friends had more in common and found it easier to be together. Relating to one's friends today is far more complex.

You are known by the company you keep. So be careful — if you are a submissive, quiet sort of chap but somehow managed to get friendly with the rowdy guys of the campus — you will be mistaken for one of them. Always remember, one good apple among the bad ones ends up getting spoilt itself.

Cutivating Charm

A charming person exudes friendship, warmth, bonhomie and fellowship around him. Charm is a way of evoking a positive response from others without having asked for it. It is this and other endearing qualities that cast their spell upon us when we come into contact with 'charming' individuals. We bask in their company and are drawn towards their magnetic personalities. What exactly is that undefinable quality that makes some people more endearing than others? Their poise, elegance, grace or a good sense of humour? These qualities may no doubt help but they are not essential pre-requisites in a charming person. Then, is it physical charm? Need one be strikingly beautiful or dashingly handsome to be charming? Certainly not. In fact, many beautiful people are not at all charming. On the other hand, many plain, simple persons can be disarmingly charming.

Charming people appear to be naturally gifted. But charm can certainly be cultivated. And who wouldn't like to cultivate it? It doesn't take much to cultivate charm. A good knowledge of human behaviour and a fine sense of dealing with the situations around, is all that goes into it.

Imagine yourself to be a man and that as you were entering the elevator of a bank building, you saw a lady walking very fast towards it in an effort to get in before the door closed. You kept the button pressed till she entered the elevator. Inside, while she is trying to regain her composure, her bag falls down. You pick it up for her. She asks you to press the eighth floor button. Although you've already done so (since that is where you get off too), you nevertheless press it again. When the elevator stops at the eighth floor, you allow her to precede you. You both head for the same door. You hold the door open for her and enter only after she has gone in. Later, you meet her in the waiting lounge where only one chair is empty. You offer it to her.

From the look on her face, it is evident that she is thoroughly charmed by your behaviour. Long after you leave the bank, you will leave behind a good impression, causing her to spontaneously murmur: 'How charming!'.

Class

What exactly is class? Here we are not talking of class as in any school or college. Class is a highly elusive quality like 'charm'. It is marked by a quiet stamp of authority, a binding presence and a bearing that announces your good breeding and refined taste. Who is said to have class? An executive in a chauffeur-driven Mercedes; intellectuals; celebrities? Class is much more than the public school syndrome with which it is usually confused. A good accent, diction, decent clothes, poise, intellect and fame do help, but do not constitute 'class' by themselves.

To determine whether you have class or not, you should ask yourself two questions. Are you able to carry yourself naturally without an iota of effort; and secondly, is it the people you meet who talk about your having class or vice versa? Always remember, those who are devoid of class continuously remind themselves and others of their possessing an abundance of it. There are individuals who talk of their most recent trip abroad to virtually anybody and everybody they meet. They will dwell on the restaurants and shopping arcades they visited, boast of their top connections, their imported household goods, etc., etc. Sounds familiar, doesn't it? This obviously is not class. Class is something which sets you a breed apart. Your modesty, honesty, good manners, politeness, sincerity towards relationships, genuine concern towards fellow human beings is more effective than any expensive material trappings to be eligible for that phrase 'a class apart'.

Road Sense

You couldn't eat your breakfast today. You were getting late for an early appointment. Look, there is a vendor near a red light selling *pao-bhaji*. But you can't stop suddenly like this in the middle of the road disrupting all the traffic around you. Indicate your intention to stop and then do so by the side of the road. Now you can buy your *pao-bhaji*. Stand aside and eat it and let the others like you take their turn. Do not eat while walking — remember, it's bad manners.

Your behaviour in the car or on the road is very important. If you are driving a vehicle, you are expected to know and above all follow traffic rules. Don't wait for the traffic police to *challan* you and show you the sign 'YOU'RE NOT A BULL. DON'T CHARGE WHEN YOU SEE RED.'

Honking, though not a crime, is as bad as having committed one. So don't honk unnecessarily. Also, don't try to attract a person's attention by the incessant blowing of your horn. Chances are, the whole neighbourhood, except for him, would be out. What about him? Well, he would be too ashamed to show his face to anyone, for having such an ill-mannered friend like you. Don't drive like a maniac on the road. You may give someone the fright of his life if, when speeding at 100 km/hr, you brake screechingly merely an inch away from him — only to ask for some directions. He would prefer to send you to the nearest police station.

Don't try to overtake another vehicle unless there is sufficient room to do so. First honk, get a clear signal, then go.

You must be thinking, what rubbish! These are only traffic rules. But it is not just that. These are all part of your behaviour pattern which, in time, becomes a part of your personality.

Enemies of Etiquette and Manners

We know very well what good manners are and the kind of good behaviour that is expected of us. But human nature is such that at times everything is shadowed by its one weakness — anger.

Anger: Anger in fact, is a common weakness which blinds you towards the good and bad, and the right and wrong. Even very civilized, well-behaved people can be found screaming and lashing out at others using the most obscene of language. How many times we have heard stories of famous film stars getting involved in a brawl just like that; or a politician finding himself in a police station, after having given in to his anger. So if you want to save your reputation, keep your temper in check. A very good antidose to it is — as soon as you feel your nerves are getting tense, take a deep breath and count to... well, 10, 20, ... 100. It depends on the intensity of your anger. Another good and easy (may not be so at that time) way out is — just turn around and make a graceful exit.

An apology after a showdown is a must to clear your heart but the best way is to prevent the showdown itself, while there is still time.

Do's and Don'ts

Respect your friends and friendship. Be natural in your dealing with others, don't be a show-off or pseudo.

Observe good manners even while on the road, like slowing down at zebra crossings, avoiding puddles so as not to splash passersbys, and not parking your vehicle just anywhere, blocking another's way.

HI ... HELLO!

"I'm Fzzzzz B zzzzz ... "
"Sorry, I couldn't get you!"
"I zzaid I'm Fzzzz Bzzzz ..."
"What's that?"
"Za'z my zame."
"What?"
"Fzzz Bzzz..."
"Mr Fzzz Bzzz ..."
"Zezz"
"Buzz off"

Introduction
Clarity should be the base of verbal introductions and referring to people. The general etiquette is straightforward: a man is introduced to a woman: the junior person between those of the same sex is introduced to the senior member. If a person introduces himself, he says as much, adding his first name and surname without a prefix. Sometimes, we tend to hope that the parties know one another and

require no formal introduction. In a situation where the name of a person escapes the recollections of the introducer, one device is to turn to that person expectantly in an unspoken request to name themselves. On occasions when someone forgets your name, it is polite to jump in with a straightforward self-identification, making no reference to the lapse.

Business Introduction

Business introductions have become less rigid in recent years.

When introducing two peers to each other, say; "Seema Sharma, this is Anil Agarwal," or "Anil Agarwal, I would like you to meet Rohan Seth."

A man is generally presented to a woman; in business, this is definitely true if she holds a more prestigious position than he does. When a secretary, or administrative assistant, male or female, is introduced to a superior, however, he or she is presented to the superior. This means you say the superior's name first as follows: "Mr Agarwal, I would like to introduce Seema Sharma, my administrative assistant." In an informal office, the introduction might be: "Anil Agarwal, I would like you to meet Seema Sharma, my administrative assistant." If you are introducing a new employee to fellow workers, it is nice to add a statement about the new person, "Manoj Verma, I would like you to meet Rahul Pathak, who will be working with you in accounting."

Acknowledging an Introduction

There is really only one appropriate way to acknowledge an introduction and that is to say, very simply "How do you do." Try not to say, "Pleased to meet," "My pleasure," or "Pleased to make your acquaintance," all statements that may not be true ten minutes after you meet someone, especially in a business atmosphere.

In the Family

When introducing members of the family to new acquaintances, it is usual to mention any kinship ties. For example, "May I introduce my husband, Vivek?" "This is my wife, Anu." "I would like you to meet my son-in-law, Roshan.", or "Vinod, this is my daughter, Rina."

Instead of the customary 'ladies first', it is better to introduce men first. However, occasionally the roles are reversed as in: 'This is Anupam Bhattacharya and his gorgeous wife Kiran... she has all the money, right Kiran?"

A chuckle and you've made yourself clear and yet managed to keep to the rules by introducing the man first.

The etiquette of making introductions has become less rigid in recent years and could be due to the more casual styles prevailing among us.

You have gone to a party. You are sipping your Campa Cola when the host comes up to you with a girl of your age and says, "Rekha, I would like you to meet Renu Chaudhary." There is a mutual exchange of greetings and after a few minutes of polite talk, you both turn back to your respective groups. But what actually happened was that the names were lost in a splutter. You didn't catch it and in all probability, neither did she.

It often happens in social gatherings that in the course of numerous introductions, you end up not remembering who's who. But cheer up, there is nothing wrong with your memory. People to whom you have been introduced are also sailing in the same boat. On a second meeting, if you go 'Ummm...', she too is likely to stammer, 'I... well...'.

So instead of beating around the bush, the best way is to be straightforward and simply say something like, "I am sorry but when we were being introduced, I didn't catch your name." Don't worry, she won't be offended and will quite willingly oblige you.

How to Introduce

To avoid such situations where neither of the parties catches each other's name, remember to pronounce names and surnames clearly to toss in a remark or two about them — like their profession, hobbies, etc. These are safe conversation openers.

Introducing Others

In a formal gathering: *You:* Mr Bhatia, meet Mr Gulati, a college friend of mine. He is with Modi Rubber as Finance Manager.

Mr Bhatia: How do you do.

In an informal gathering: You take a friend along to the group.

You: "This is Sudhir."

and then indicating each person go on... "This is Radhika, Ramesh, Ruchika..." and so on.

From those being introduced, a mere hello will suffice. After the formal introduction, somebody should draw the newcomer into the conversation by asking him a simple question like: 'What do you do?' or 'Have you been in Delhi for long?'

At a wedding: In a marriage function, the introductions should be done with context to the groom and the bride.

You: "Mrs Agarwal, this is Mrs Gupta, the bride's *mausi*. She also lives in Calcutta." Instead of "How do you do", the greeting here may be in the form of *'namaste'* or a mere nod of the head, indicating acknowledgement of the greeting.

Mrs Agarwal: "How nice. I also belong to Calcutta. Where do you stay in Calcutta?"

In college: You are walking along with a friend and happen to spot another friend unknown to the person you are with.

Excuse yourself by saying, "I won't be a minute"; or you could introduce them both to each other.

You: "Sudhir, meet Randhir, an old friend of mine. We were together in school."

Sudhir (friend): "Hello, how do you do."

Randhir (stranger):"Hello."

Introducing Yourself

Introducing oneself is much more difficult because here you are totally on your own and the other person is an absolute stranger to you.

At a formal party: It is better if the host introduces you but if he does not, then the best way is to use your business card. Hand it to the other person and say "Hello, I am Aneesh Gupta, Business Manager for Bharat Ltd."

Never ask for the other person's introduction without giving yours first. If you are an extrovent and enjoy making friends, go up to a person and introduce yourself by saying something like "Hello, I'm Ramesh Bhandari..." and set the ball rolling.

To a celebrity: You are invited to a party and to your good luck, you find your favourite actor, Amitabh Bachchan also there. If no one introduces you to him, you can directly go up to him and introduce yourself: "Hello, I'm Ashok Malhotra, an old fan of yours...". Most likely, Amitabh will acknowledge it gracefully and you may even ask for an autograph or a photograph with him, if you so desire.

In an office: You go to an office to meet Mr R.K. Sharma whom you have never met before. The best way is to walk up to the reception and enquire about him.

You: "Excuse me, I want to see Mr R.K. Sharma, the Assistant Sales Manager".

Receptionist: "May I know your name, please?"

You: "I'm Ashok Rana from Bharat Sales."

Receptionist: "Kindly wait, I'll inform him."

If there is no reception around, you can walk up to the first person you see and enquire: "Excuse me, I'm here to meet Mr R.K. Sharma. Would you be able to help me?"

Reply: "You can go inside. He's in his office."

Once you have been able to locate Mr. Sharma's whereabouts, go up to him and introduce yourself.

You: "Mr Sharma?"

Mr Sharma: "Yes."

You: "Hello, I'm Ashok Rana from Bharat Sales...".

Come to the point right away. Don't start telling him how long it took you to locate him.

Introducing Children

When it comes to children, we find ourselves at a loss as to how to teach them to greet others. Children are shy and feel very self-conscious when introduced to others. Parents introduce their children to others in one of the following ways; Either the paretns will go on persuading the child (in front of the visitor) to greet the visitor (they can even be found threatening him like "I will not take you to the market if you do not say hello to Uncle") while the shy child would make every possible effort to bury his face in his mother's lap. In the other case, parents will leave the child out of introductions to the guests, ignoring him totally, not realizing that this may give the child an inferiority complex. Both these approaches are wrong. In the first case, the child is getting undesirable extra attention with the result that he becomes self-conscious and withdraws in his shell. In the second case, he is totally ignored. Since he has not been taught to greet people, he flounders. The child should be introduced to the visitor as a member of your family when the other introductions are being made. This not only makes him feel important, giving him an individual identity but at the same time gives him a sense of belonging.

Do not launch into a detailed description of his achievements, most recent activities, etc. Not only will this embarrass the child but bore the listeners.

As he sees others exchanging greetings, he imitates them. Try this a few times and you will never find him hiding behind a curtain whenever he is next called out to be introduced.

EXTENDING GREETINGS

*'It dates back to the era of Cavemen.
Hands were extended to show that they were empty
a la handshake today.
With the only difference that it was a
sword in those times,
today it may be a remote control device
for that bomb planted under your seat.'*

A smile is the most beautiful part of one's personality. You can make friends by a mere smile. And why not? Who wouldn't like to be friend a person with a smiling face? A smile exudes warmth. We greet our friends, relatives, acquaintances and superiors not only at the first meeting of the day but often repeatedly at brief intervals throughout the day. Thus, a smile creates and confirms the warmth in the relations without having to utter a word. It is a consent to friendly contact.

The manner in which persons greet each other varies from place to place. But greeting people at least the first time you see them each day is a polite custom. For the rest of the day, you can make do with a smile. Do not force yourself to smile as its artificiality is evident at once.

Often people are shy and they may be waiting for the other person to take the lead in greeting them. Well, there is no harm even if you are their superior. It will only enhance your image in their eyes. So always be prepared to intitiate a greeting. Because it is these little things in life that eventually blossom into lasting relationships. A warm greeting, besides breaking the veneer of formality, spells goodwill.

There are several forms of greeting — a friendly smile, a nod, a wink, a handshake, a kiss and most common in our surroundings — a *namaste*.

Verbal greetings

'Hello' is the universal verbal form of greeting which is acceptable in most situations — even strangers say Hello in passing. A more modern and popular usage is 'Hi'. Both these are said with a smile on the lips and a slight nod of head. A reply to these can either be a plain Hi or Hello or if you wish, you can use the added pleasantry "How are you"? It is often used as a gambit to start off the conversation.

Now starting a conversation does not necessarily mean that you should take the other person's words literally by reciting a long detailed list of your physical and mental ailments or your financial problems.

The response to "How are you?" should be "Fine, thank you, how are you?" and nothing more than this.

Shaking Hands

People shake hands more frequently today than they did years ago. Today, the handshake has come to be the most accepted form of greeting and occurs in the most varied cultural areas of the world with a few exceptions. The Japanese, for instance, do not shake hands; they bow and the depth of the bow is generally related to the degree of respect due to the person being greeted. In India,

the traditional form of greeting elders is touching their feet and saying 'namaste' with folded hands. However, with modernization and the influx of western culture, these forms of greeting are not the rule everywhere.

There is more to a handshake than a flick of the wrist or the press of a palm. A handshake can reveal our hidden personality traits. Nobody likes a handshake that feels like a jellyfish or a vice-like grip that makes you wince. A firm but smooth grip is considered the best handshake. It gives a message of warmth and friendliness to the other person. In a sense, it seems to be saying: "You can depend upon me."

Handshaking usually accompanies all expressions of greeting, farewells, gratitude, congratulations, introductions, etc. When formally joining or departing from groups, it is customary to shake every individual's hands.

Namaste

Our country has the best answer to a greeting — the *namaste*. In large gatherings, one is saved the trouble of shaking (and experiencing) varied handshakes. The *namaste* symbolizes a welcome and reflects our traditional hospitality and service to others. And this is what makes it the most unique form of greeting in the world.

Some time back even The Times of London praised the *namaste* as a simple yet graceful and reticent Indian gesture of greeting. It further added, 'Today in Britain and elsewhere, by constantly wringing and kneading one another's hands during handshakes, many people worldwide often nurse sore thumbs and swollen wrists. In fact, many heads of state, politicians and even executives deliberately tone down the firmness of their otherwise warm handshakes. If only they could adopt and accept *Namaste* in place of handshake, we are sure they would be better off.'

Touching the Feet

This kind of greeting is only used by the young as a mark of respect to their elders. It is the traditional form of greeting in Indian culture.

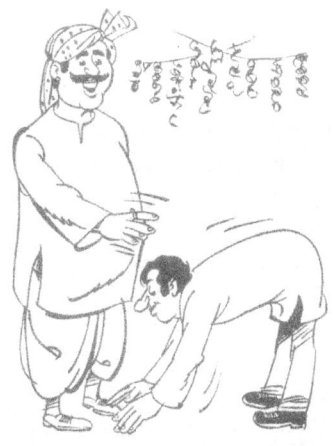

Young people bow down and touch the feet of their elders, who in turn bestow them with blessings like *'Jeete raho'*, *'Khush raho'*, etc.

Who would dare emulate the greeting of the *Masai* tribe of A rica? On meeting one another, they spit and get spat back at!

Informal Greetings

This is the age of informal greetings and behaviour. But this does not mean that our friends should be greeted with thumps on their backs or subjected to nose-tweaking to signify our ready affection. It may instead keep them a mile away from you. If you want to exhibit your affection, a peck on the cheek should suffice. You may even resort to a friendly pat on the shoulder.

Greeting Someone on Entering

Men stand when they are introduced to each other. It is acceptable, however, for a woman to remain sitting when a man is presented to her. It is gracious to stand to greet anyone who comes into your house, office or any gathering with, of course, the exception of servants, co-workers or assistants who come in regularly.

Always stand to greet a visitor or when an exchange of handshakes or a *namaste* or maybe even a mere Hi-Hello takes place.

As soon as you have finished the greetings, invite the visitor to sit down and make himself comfortable.

How Children Should Greet their Elders

This is a question parents ask themselves when they begin teaching their child to greet others. Should the child be taught to say *namaste*, or hello; to shake hands or touch the feet? Since the child cannot differentiate between the variety of people you entertain, he must be properly guided.

Start with teaching him only one way of greeting. In a joint family, a boy can be taught to touch his elders' feet. However, in some families, as girls are not allowed to do this before marriage, they may be taught to say *namaste*.

If you are the type that entertains friends very often, your child may be taught to say a polite 'Hello'.

A child looks very sweet, shaking hands with the guests, but not every child is willing to do it, so instead of embarrassing yourself and torturing the poor little by repeatedly coaxing him to go and shake hands with the guests, just stick to a 'hello', which the child will find much safer and will conform to easily.

Leave-taking, Dismissing or Escorting Someone

Leave-taking is also a part and parcel of greetings. By a gracious leave-taking of the person we have met, we only succeed in strengthening the bonds of friendship for the future. One has to use one's discretion to judiciously round up a conversation and take leave of the other. 'Bye', 'See you', 'Till next time then', 'I shall take leave of you now', etc. are some standard accepted norms used when parting company.

You can dismiss someone by simply nodding or thanking them. If the other person is taking leave, stand up and escort him to the main door. Then greet him accordingly as you greeted him when he entered.

A handshake or 'Hi' or a simple 'Bye' or 'See you soon' will also suffice. Or you may prefer to say *namaste* or touch the person's feet (depending on your relationship). Do not forget to ask them to come again and to keep in touch.

Important visitors require red-carpet welcome. It is gracious to walk the person to his car or whatever mode of transport he has.

If you are expecting a person, do not make them wait for too long.

Similarly, in an office, never allow an important visitor to find his own way out alone. If your office is a maze of corridors, extend this courtesy to even the most ordinary visitors.

Making Enquiries

At some point of time or the other, all of us have felt the need for establishing contact with total strangers for making certain enquiries. It may be in an office, seeking information or on the road for directions.

Good manners demand that we greet a person before proceeding to make our request, at least with a genuine smile. And don't forget, a simple "Thank you" after your doubts have been cleared.

CONVERSATION—MIND THAT LANGUAGE

There is no point in using time that could be spent on the polo field speaking to some idiot with nothing to offer but the time of day. Get right to the point. You've got no time to talk about the weather.

'What do you do?'
'I'm in steel.'
'Is that steel as in 'stainless' or steal as in 'blind'?'
A quick follow-up is needed.
'How's your profit margin?'
'Around two million.'
'A year?'
'No, a week.'
Forget polo – now you can talk about the weather.

*U*nless you are remarkably eloquent, which few of us are, your manner of speech will not be a cause for comment. But if you speak poorly or mess around with your native language, this will indeed be noticed. Speaking is idiosyncratic. It is a reflection of learned patterns of talking and personality. Poor speech may grate on the ears of others but is tolerated by all but the very blunt and outspoken in polite society.

Speaking Skills

The first rule of speaking is: if you can't do it well, do something to remedy the situation. Take the help of 'Do-it-yourself' courses designed to help improve speech. Or get a friend to point out the errors of your speech. A good way to know whether you have a communication problem is observing your listeners reaction to you.

A long-winded person soon makes everyone in the room uncomfortable. Besides frequently being and often rudely interrupted, he is rarely listened to with close attention.

If you are talking too fast or too slow or in an accent that is hard to understand — your listeners may ask you to repeat something several times or tell you at a later point that they missed a part of what you had said earlier. These will give you indications that your speech delivery is somewhat erroneous. Poor grammar or misuse of a word is more difficult to detect since the polite refrain from reacting negatively to such errors. The only remedy for this problem is by listening to the speech of others and see how yours differs.

When analyzing the effect your spoken words have on others, if you find that you are getting more negative signals, take them as an indication that a little self-improvement is in order.

Listening

Listening to others is an art in itself and an integral part of etiquette. Listening is a supreme compliment to a speaker. It nevers fails to reap benefits for the listener. Focus your attention on the person who is speaking and do not interrupt. Look the speaker directly in the eye most of the time. Lean slightly forward if you are sitting to indicate interest. And if possible, sit close to the speaker.

Certain gestures of the listener reveal moments when their attention has been caught unequivocally. They may take off their glasses when the conversation takes a particularly fascinating turn or may lean forward in their chair as if not to miss a single word or cup their chin in their palm and fix unwavering attention and unblinking eyes on the speaker.

Above all, when you are listening to someone, do not look as if you are mentally planning what you want to say next. As a listener, you are expected to react to what you are hearing. Body language, nods or an emphatic shake of the head at appropriate moments reveal more than words. Slip in phrases like "I agree completely," or "You are absolutely right on that point", or "Quite true".

If you disagree with the point being made, you might say, "I'll have to give that some more thought," or even simply, "I'm not sure I agree with you on that point".

Perhaps the subtlest statement ever heard along these lines is, "You may be right". Spoken in just the right tone, this statement carries the silent implication, "But I doubt it".

Conversational Starters

Starting a conversation with your friends and acquaintances is not a hurdle. It is only when you are introduced to a stranger that you are at a temporary loss for words.

Let's assume that you've gone to a party and have just been introduced to a stranger. In such a situation, it is always desirable to initiate a conversation on a general topic. For example:

"Where are you working?"

"I'm with Hindustan Lever."

If you are familiar with any latest business happenings in that particular organization, you can expand further on these lines. If not, you can still go on to talk about safe and general topics like films, sports, politics, the weather, etc. For example:

"Have you been in Delhi long?" or

"Oh, it's so hot today!" or

"What a coincidence that you are also fond of gardening! That's my favourite pastime too."

If it is an intimate gathering where people know each other well, any topic under the sun may be broached. But keep in mind that whatever you talk of must be of interest to everyone. Jokes and anecdotes come quite handy at such occasions. Try to refrain from talking shop. This can only be of interest when it is an interdepartment office party. Not when there is only a handful of people from the same organization or line of profession present in the group.

If it is a courtesy visit you are paying to your grandparents or uncles, aunts or some other elderly family friends, the conversation automatically follows an altogether different pattern. As you belong to a different age and era, your elderly relations have fixed opinions about certain things. It is better to let them do most of the talking, usually starting with a 'In our days...'. Don't let it bother you. Just remember, the time when you hark back to 'your' days is not very far either.

Even if you disagree on certain points, it is disrespectful to criticize old people. Even though you know they are wrong, do not try to urge your point home and give cause for offence. It is safer to ostensibly agree with them.

Using Flattery Wisely

There is an art to flattering someone. Flattery can be done in two ways:

(a) To compliment excessively and often insincerely, especially in order to win the favour of someone.

(b) To portray someone favourably.

When going about the business of flattering someone, make very sure that you follow the second mode. False flattery rarely sounds like anything but what it is.

Another commonly followed mode of flattery is by complimenting a person. You like the tie someone is wearing, and you tell him so simply and briefly. A colleague is carrying an especially handsome leather purse; again, you tell her so pleasantly and briefly. These little compliments on another's tastes not only makes them feel good, but also puts you in their good books forever. You just have to be a little careful not to overdo the amount of flattery and to continue sounding authentic.

A more intensive form of flattery should still be honest, while having a definite motive.

If, for example, your friend wrote a good article which has been published in *The Times of India,* do not say: "That article you wrote was really dynamite. Just marvelous. How do you do it?"

Instead, with a little thought, something better and more realistic like this can be said "Your article in *The TOI* was very impressive. Especially that point you made about future developments." With this compliment, you have shown your appreciation of the article and reflection on it.

Avoiding Slang

Slang is often used when talking with your peer group. Your elders and other family friends and superiors in your place of work should be given the respect due to them by keeping slang out of your speech.

Slang often displays a sense of belonging — to define who is out and who is in — specially at the college level. Taken to extremes, this is rude behaviour. Remember abusive and swear slang vocabulary should not be a part of a ladies' conversation. Even when in a temper, keep your tongue under control.

Art of Conversation and Your Child

It is very important to inculcate the art of conversation in children. They learn a lot by observing. How you converse with others is keenly observed by your little one and then imitated to the letter.

For a child, the first rule for a good conversation should be politeness and respect to others. Be it elders or his peer group, he should be taught the correct manner of speech.

Slang should be kept out of 'polite' conversation. Keep a watch out for any use of swear words or cursing in your child's speech. An immediate stop should be put to bad language.

They should also be taught not to intervene while two persons are talking. They should wait for them to finish before saying what he has to. Polite words like, Please, Thank you, Excuse me, Bye, Hello, How do you do, Sorry, etc. should be made an essential part of his speech and he should use them frequently and appropriately.

Sarcasm, Humour, Double Meanings

The above three in a conversation can be destructive if misused. Don't make uncalled-for wisecracks at a gathering or party unless you know the people very well and know that your comments will not be taken amiss. Refrain from double-edged ambiguous statements and keep your sarcasm and deadly wit for intimate gatherings.

Dirty jokes must be taken out of the closet only when two or three good friends are together and that too only in male company. Men should not insult the presence of a lady by relating vulgar jokes. A lady on the other hand should not give rise to unsavoury gossip by telling these jokes herself. There are many funny jokes that can be said without being crude or vulgar.

Modulating Your Voice

Modulation refers to the rhythm and tonal quality of your voice. It is specially important not to talk too loudly. If you are at an intimate romantic lunch, it would be embarassing if the whole restaurant got to know your boyfriend has just proposed to you.

On the other hand, a voice that is too soft and can barely be heard will fail to make an impact of any sort. In fact, an extremely soft voice can make one appear weak and ineffective.

So all those who want to be respected and listened to should make an effort to maintain a well-modulated voice most of the time. Also make sure that your voice, while being pleasant, is loud enough to be understood.

Filling Those Gaps

A good conversationalist does not dominate a conversation but permits others to have their say as well. But at times, there may be such gaps in between the conversation when one doesn't know what to do and what to say. Pitch in when conversation begins to flag or trails to a halt. Subtle approaches are always best. A change of topic often helps in filling those gaps. So does calling a person's attention to what had been said earlier.

Accepting Criticism Graciously

Fault-finding and criticism is an irritating trait in many people. They delight in tearing others to pieces. No doubt, at times some people need and deserve criticism, but it should be done mildly and above all, constructively. Just telling somebody he is stupid, dumb and is doing something wrong not only turns that person into your biggest enemy but also demoralizes him. So be liberal in your encouragement. Instead, let the person know you have faith in his ability, that he has an untapped flair for it. The odds are he will put in his optimum effort in order to excel and please you.

Similarly, if you ever find yourself criticized, do not take it to heart. Take it in good faith and try to locate your fault and rectify it.

In fact, it is always better to keep criticism out of the general conversation. Instead, call a person aside and say what you have to privately.

Practising — A Final Word

Finally, the key to improving your speaking skills is practice. Watch others, and when you hear something that appeals to you, some phrase you think will work for you — adopt it in your speech.

It is true that poised speech is a sign of good manners and is one of the graces that anyone can acquire without too much effort.

TELEPHONE MANNERS

Tring, tring.
"Hello."
"This is ABC Refrigerator. Is your referigerator running?"
"No, it is very much in the same place as it has been standing for the past six years. Ha, ha, ha!"
Slam ... click.

Timing
As a general rule, telephone calls to a household should not be made before 7 A.M. and after 11 P.M. However, there are many exceptions to the rule, depending upon who's calling whom and if it is an emergency.

Answering the Phone
A commonly accepted way of answering the phone is 'Hello'. In fact, that is all that needs to be said, but some like to announce their telephone number or their name as in '...6415911' or 'Sharma here'.

Staff in a big household sometimes announce the name of the residence quite like in an office:

'Burman House, Good Morning.'

In an office, it is customary to first greet the caller and then tell the name of the company. As soon as the telephone operator picks up the phone, she is expected to say:

"Good morning, Pasupati Acrylon", or "Good afternoon, Modi Rubber."

This way the caller knows he has dialled the correct number and he can immediately come to the point.

Identification

Announce your identity as soon as you know you have got through to the correct number.

If it's a personal call, you are likely to be familiar with all the family members. So ask after the well-being of the person on the line and then go on to ask for whomever you wish to speak to. The conversation will probably be as follows.

Receiver—"Hello."

You—"Is that 2415673?"

Rec.—"Yes."

You—"I'm Ruchika this side. May I know who's on the line?"

Rec.—"Hi Ruchika. I'm Radha."

You—"Hello Didi (since you know Radha is your friend's elder sister) How are you?"

Radha—"Fine, thank you. And how are you? Haven't seen you for a long time."

You—"Yeah, just busy with the studies. Didi, how is Reema? Is she around?"

Radha—"Yeah, yeah, she is here. I'll just call her, hold on for a minute."

She calls her younger sister with whom you can then chat.

Returning Calls

If the telephone call is mistakenly cut off, whoever made the call in the first place should call back. In case you were out or not free to speak at that particular moment and the caller leaves a message for you, then it is your duty to return the call.

Wrong Number

If you have dialled a wrong number (which happens very often) do not slam the phone down. You should apologize to whoever answered the call. If you answer the phone, and it is a wrong number, do not be rude. Just tell the caller "Sorry, you've got the wrong number" politely and ring off. If you persistently get wrong calls, do not take your frustration out on the other party. Instead, either ask the telephone exchange to get you the number or put the phone down and wait for some time before trying again.

Similarly, if you are at the receiving end of wrong numbers, tell them politely for the first few times, or else keep your phone off the hook for a few minutes. This may help the caller get the correct line, and you some peace.

Messages

Good message-takers are a boon to any office. The proper way of taking a message is by writing down the name of the caller, his number and the message clearly and accurately on a piece of paper. Leave this message where the recepient is most likely to see it.

Long Conversations

They are better avoided. Not only does it increase your telephone bill, it may also be an inconvenience to other people who are trying to get through to you, perhaps with an urgent message.

Ending a Phone Conversation

Even if both of you are great talkers, one has to tire first. Ideally, the best way is to wait for a pause in the flow and say something like:

'Sorry dear, but I have to cut it short ...'.

With some acceptable excuse like guests have come or the doorbell is ringing or the child is crying. Don't slam down the receiver on the caller when he is speaking. It is the height of rudeness. After you have conveyed your inability to continue the conversation, say 'I'll call you again soon' or 'Give me a call sometime'. This should be followed by the customary 'Bye, bye' or 'Be good, hope to see you soon' etc. This could be a definite indication of the end of a conversation.

Children on the Phone

Children love the telephone. The ringing of the phone is fascinating for a child. But this habit should not be encouraged. Unless your child is old enough to hold a conversation and take down the message, he should not be allowed to pick up the phone. At the same time, give him the occasional chance to converse over a phone in your presence. Teach him how to hold a conversation such as how to say hello, your telephone number, calling the concerned person and taking down the message. Slowly and gradually, he will master the technique.

Do not allow him to misuse the telephone. Picking up the receiver unnecessarily or dialling aimlessly, punching out numbers at random or stretching the cord around will not only damage the instrument but also keep your line engaged unnecessarily.

Answering Machine

Answering machines are the latest fad in our country and are gaining popularity because of their various uses. An answering machine is a device attached to the telephone instrument like an audio cassette and is used to record telephone messages in your absence.

All that you have to do is to switch on the machine before going out. If someone calls in your absence, they will be answered by a recorded message: "This is K. Mehta's residence. He is not at home right now. Please leave a message after the beep." The caller is now supposed to leave the message.

Try to be as brief as possible while talking to an answering machine. Just leave your name, call-back number and urgency of the matter on the tape. With an answering machine, you can be sure that the message will be received accurately.

WRITTEN COMMUNICATION

The moment we speak or write a few lines, it reveals more of ourselves than we may care to admit. Since the use of language is one of the chief yardsticks by which people evaluate others, we must try to be as much in command of our personal communication system as possible.

Our written communication reveals as much of ourselves as our spoken words: "A letter is simply talk upon paper." As this is one of the chief yardsticks by which people evaluate us, you should try to be well in command of your personal communications system. Written communication is a matter of common courtesy and you should be concerned about how your method and manner of communication will affect others.

When you write a letter, you enter into a personal relationship with the reader. Now it is up to you whether you turn it into a jubilant, warm and friendly one or make it dull and dreary.

Is Writing a Chore?

Neither writing nor reading a letter should be viewed as a chore. Reluctant correspondents, to whom the art of letter-writing does not come naturally, will find their task easier if they work out what they want to say and how they wish to say it, before attempting to write a letter.

Letter Writing Formula

Simple and clear : The secret of writing a good letter lies in its being simple and clear. Just like one friend talking to another, a letter should sound like a good conversation. It should be straightforward, meaningful and written with a fixed purpose.

Salutation: The greeting to the reader with which every letter begins is called the salutation.

In a business or formal letter, it is

Dear Sir/Madam

If you want to give it a personal touch, write

Dear Miss Gandhi/ Mr Juneja

Never use 'Respected Sir/Madam' unless you are writing to a high dignitary or perhaps to the principal of your school. In an informal letter, the salutation begins with 'Dear' or 'My dear...' followed by the first name of the person, e.g. My dear Manoj or Dear Radha.

Making a good impression: The impression a letter makes on the reader depends on presentation as well as on content. Spelling and grammar should be watched, but in most private correspondence, a natural and personal flow of words is preferable. Faulty spelling is not acceptable except for the most private correspondence. Crossing out and the occasional inkblot are also excusable only in personal letters.

A letter set out nicely in the middle of the page, with wide margins, is pleasing to behold. Sufficient space between the lines, which should be even, is also pleasing to the reader.

Try and be as legible as possible. If your writing is hard to decipher, rely on a typewriter. To lend a personal note to typewritten letters, you can write the opening 'Dear so -and-so' and sign off with a pen.

Signatures to all letters are in the writer's hand.

Body

The body of a letter is where business is conducted.

Business letter: In a business letter, which is quite brief (rarely longer than one page, while most limit themselves to one or two paragraphs), one should come to the point directly. It is always better to be straightforward than beat around the bush.

Please note that 'short' does not mean that you adopt a shorthand or telegraphic style, leaving all your prepositions out. For example:

"Recd ltr Dec. 8. Will advise no later than one week."

This will do for a telegram but not a letter. Even in today's fast-paced world, this method is not adopted in a letter. Be sure every sentence is complete in itself and logical.

In a business letter, if you are writing on behalf of your company, use the first person as 'we' but when you are responding to a business letter in your personal capacity, use 'I' wherever possible.

"We are in receipt of your letter of 25.6.92 wherein..." (corporate basis).

"I am in receipt of your letter..." (individual capacity).

Personal letter: The body of a personal letter can include anything, depending upon your relationship and what you wish to convey. There is no set formula or prescription in writing a personal letter. A few broad guidelines may be suggested.

A general way of starting a personal letter to the following.

Friend:
My Dear Sheela,

Hello, I hope this letter finds you in the pink of health and spirits....

Elders:
Respected chachaji,

Namaste,

Hope this letter finds you in the best of health and spirits... .

A child :
My dear Tinny Minny,

How are you ? I received your lovely card only yesterday. It was real sweet of you to remember my birthday....

Closure

In the last para of the letter, you may if you wish stress once again anything that you have already written. It should motivate the reader into doing what you want him to do. It should also contain your farewell and the hope of hearing from the other party.

The closure, like the salutation, is a matter of custom and a polite way of concluding a letter. Expressions used must suit the tone of the letter and match the salutations which will be based on the relationship between the parties. The closure must be simple.

Business: In a business letter, about the most formal closing ever used today is:

Thanking you,

Yours faithfully,

Sd
Name of person
Designation

There is no need to write the name of the company or its address if you are using the official letter head. (This is when you have been using 'we' all along on the corporate level.)

When you use the 'Dear Sir/ Madam' address, sign off as 'Yours faithfully'. In case you address the person by name as

'Dear Mr Sharma', sign off as 'Yours sincerely'. If writing a business letter in an individual capacity, and having used 'I' throughout the letter, the closing should be:

With best/kind regards,

Yours sincerely.

'Yours obediently' should be kept only for those sick-leave letters to your school principal.

Personal: A personal letter can have any closing remark, depending upon your relations with the person.

Friends and peers: With lots of love, Yours sincerely,

or

Bye-bye for now, hope to see you soon,

Use 'Yours lovingly' only in case you are writing to your parents.

Elder relatives: With kind regards/Your (nephew/niece or whatever the relation is). If you do not wish to spell out the exact relationship, just write *'Yours affectionately'* and sign your name below.

Elders to children: It's time to close the letter. Now be good, take care. Convey my regards to your mom and dad.'

Yours lovingly,

Chintu *mama* or Radhika *mausi*

Consistency: The salutations should match their closures:

Salutations	Closures	Remarks
Dear Sir/ Madam	Yours faithfully	A formal letter on behalf of the company using 'we'.
Dear Miss Ram	Yours sincerely	Informal business letter written between persons known to each other using 'I'.
My dear Radha	Yours lovingly	A personal letter.

Signature : Sign legibly on any letter. Although in a personal letter, you do not write the name and designation as such, in a business letter, full name and title of the signing authority along with the name of the company should be clearly mentioned. Your signature should always be handwritten and just above the place where your name has been typed.

```
Yours faithfully,
for Modi Rubber Limited
Sign
(Ashwani Singhal) Financial Controller
```

Model Letters
General Business Letter

The ABC Corporation,
Parliament Street,
New Delhi.

Dear sir,

We are in receipt of your letter no. xyz dated 3.4.89 regarding your enquiry about our products.

In this regard, please find enclosed a set of our brochures containing the latest price list et al.

Hope it meets your requirement.

Thanking you,

Yours faithfully,
DEF Corpn Ltd,

Sd/-

(A.M. Gill)
General Manager

Letter of complaint

The Area Officer
Mahanagar Telephone Nigam Ltd,
New Delhi.

Sub: Wrong billing to phone no...for an STD call no... made to Calcutta.

Kindly refer to your bill no... dated... raised on telephone no.... To my utter amazement, I realize that I have been wrongly billed for an STD call to Calcutta code no... telephone no... for an amount of Rs 560.

I would like to add that no such STD call was made by me to Calcutta and I am absolutely unfamiliar with the Calcutta number that appears in my bill. Under the circumstances, kindly look into the matter and rectify the error at your earliest.

Thanking you,

Yours faithfully,

Sd/-

(Name, address and telephone number of the applicant.)

Letter of congratulations

My dear Rohit,

Hope this finds you in the best of health and spirits. I must first of all congratulate you on your receiving the scholarship to Hungary for three years. I was always sure that your hard work would win you this prestigious scholarship and I am glad that your efforts have been suitably rewarded now.

With warm regards and best wishes,

Yours sincerely,

Sd/-
(Rahul Ghosh)

Letter declining an invitation

Dear Arpita,

Thank you very much for your invitation to dinner next Saturday. I would have loved to be there and meet all of you, but unfortunately, I will be in Calcutta around that time, so you must please excuse me.

Meanwhile, I sincerely hope that your dinner party will be a great success. Give my love to all.

Yours affectionately,

Sd/-
(Radhika Menon)

Condolence letters

When someone dies, a letter of sympathy should be dispatched to their nearest and dearest as soon as possible. Keep the tone light and direct. Phrases such as: 'We send our heartful sympathies', or 'Please let me know if there is anything I can do', or 'We send our fondest love and thoughts to you at this time,' may be used.

Try not to write of the dead person as 'passed on' or 'passed over'. Direct reference is the best. You can write of any special memories of the dead person that the reader would like to hear about, any tribute that can be paid to their work, character or efforts.

Addressing an Envelope

Size: The envelope should neither be too big nor too small. It should be befitting the size of the letter.

Accuracy: The name and address should be exact and do spell each word correctly. Try not to use abbreviations like Bldg, St, Ave, Rd, etc. The Pincode should be given for prompt delivery.

Legibility: If typing the address, there should not be any overtyping. But if it is handwritten, do so in bold letters so that it is clear and easily readable.

Styles: There are two styles of writing addresses—Indent and Block forms:

   Mr A.K. Srivastava

(Indented form where each line is written after leaving some space.)

Mr A.K. Srivastava

(Block style where all the lines start from the same point.)

Specifications or Confidential or Personal

The words Confidential or Personal must be typed on the upper left-hand corner of the envelope or in the centre above the name.

The term Personal implies that the letter is meant for the reader alone and is not to be opened by his/her secretary. If marked Confidential, then it can be dealt with by the secretary.

Postscript

P.S. written at the base of a letter stands for 'postscript' and contains the writer's afterthoughts. The use of P.S. is wholly acceptable in most private correspondence but not in formal or official correspondence. Nor is it acceptable in a letter of condolence.

Book post: This means that the letter is sent open and not closed.

Card only: This is stictly for greeting cards etc. and not letters or any other documents. The postal charges are also lesser than for a normal letter.

UCP, Regd AD and speed post: These are different postal signs for sending a letter. You get a stamped receipt for these letters from the Post Office. It ensures speedy and confirmed delivery of the letter.

Airmail: All letters going out of the country should be marked 'Airmail'. They are weighed separately at the Post Office and stamped accordingly.

JOB HUNTING

"Job hunting? Is it the same as in tiger-hunting?"

"No way. It is much more rough and tough".

Just as holding down a job successfully often involves matters of etiquette, there are a number of conventions in applying for and getting a suitable job.

The Resume or Curriculum

What do I want to do?: Before applying for a job, you have to answer this difficult question. Sit down with a piece of paper and list the things you are proud to have achieved. Take a stock of your personal accomplishments and list your strengths and weaknesses. Leave the latter aside and concentrate on the better part of your personality, the strengths.

Once you are clear in your mind about the line of profession you wish to pursue, talk to those already in the field. Then make a curriculum or resume or biodata.

Remember this will be your advertisement for a potential job and should highlight your strenghts, merits and achievements.

Main points of a resume: A resume should be in the following form.

Name and Address: Your name and address should be stated at the outset in bold letters. Please put the address to which correspondence is to be directed. Also indicate a telephone number where you can be reached.

Father/Husband's Name: Write Mr or Shri before the name.

Date of Birth: It can either be in numerical form or in words, like 23.7.68 or 23rd July, 1968.

Educational Qualifications: This includes your academic degrees. It should be given in the reverse chronological order, stating first your last acquired degree and going backwards to the previous ones.

Professional Qualifications: If you have any professional qualifications, like a secretarial course or have done a computer course or a management diploma, all these come under this head.

Present Job and Previous Employments: Descriptions of the jobs you have held in the past and the present one should be given again in the reverse chronological order. Begin with current work experience, then go onto previous jobs. Be sure to state your present desgination and previous ones as well as job descriptions.

Extracurricular Activities: If you have been a good sportsperson, mention it separately. Any other activities like dramatics, stage shows, or NCC, etc. that you have been involved in can be mentioned here.

Hobbies: The basic difference between the former and hobbies is that the former is done on a large scale, while the latter is strictly for one's own pleasure and is done in one's leisure time.

Salary Expected: This is a negotiable clause and if it is your first or second job, leave this column out. At this stage, you require experience more than to bother about the salary.

References: Give one or two names of persons known to you who are well settled and in reliable positions and whom you know will render you good backing in case your future employer wishes to enquire about you from them.

Model Biodata

Name	:	A.S. Jain
Father's Name	:	Mr M.K. Jain
Date of Birth	:	19.9.67
Permanent Address	:	B-1/10, Mayur Vihar, New Delhi. Tel: 551234
Postal Address	:	251, Park Street, Calcutta, Tel: 4456219

Educational Qualifications	:	1. B.Com from Delhi University in the year... with I Division (aggregate may be given).
		2. XII ...
		3. X ...
Professional Qualification	:	1. CA...
		2. Six months' Computer Course...
Job Experience	:	1. The present job, with the name of the company, designation and nature of job....
		2. Previous job..... .
		3. Prior to the above... .
Extracurricular activities	:	1. Good in sports. Played hockey at district level. 2. Cricket...
Hobbies	:	Reading, writing, gardening.
Salary Expected	:	Negotiable.
References:	:	1. Mr. H.K. Mathur, General Manager, ABC Corpn, 126, Parliament Street, New Delhi-1
		2. ....

Do not give more than two or three references.

Applications

A clear, informative, well-presented letter asking for employment is definitely singled out from the usual run-of-the-mill applications.

In response to an advertisement: Keep the following in mind when replying to an advertisement.

* Ensure that if specific information is requested, you supply it.
* Check that the full name of the person to whom the correspondence is addressed is accurately spelt and also that you

have included their prefix and correct designation, such as the Personnel Director.

* The address must be accurate.

Applying for a job when there is no advertisement: When you send an unsolicited letter, it is best to address your correspondence to a specific named individual and not an anonymous Head of a Department. Applications may be sent to the Managing Director or the Personnel Manager.

Content: A letter that accompanies your resume should state whether you are replying to an advertisement (state the publication and date) and produce an interesting reason why you think you should be considered for the post. Enthusiasm for the field, aptitude for the work and aspirations to succeed, along with relevant experience or qualifications are best.

Indicate whether you are currently employed/immediately available. Do not make any reference to your present contract of employment.

Use clean white paper and write only on one side of the paper.

To type or not: Job applications are usually typewritten, but in certain cases applicants are asked to write in their own hand.

Interview

Once you have sent your biodata with the application, if the management considers you suitable for the job, you will get a call letter to appear for the interview on a particular date, at a specific time.

Punctuality is important, but arriving noticeably ahead of time suggests lack of confidence and inexperience. So give not more than 10 minute's grace. At the same time, being late for an interview not only shows discourtesy, it is also a very poor start. Once at the reception desk, give your full name and the name of the person with whom you have the appointment or you can even show your call letter.

Making a good impression: Unfair as it may be, many hopes are won or lost in the first impression, a crucial factor. During the opening stages of the interview, it is better to respond than to initiate.

Greeting: If the interviewer extends his hands, shake it warmly, otherwise just say hello with a nod. Acknowledge a smile with a smile.

Posture counts: Enter the room gracefully with shoulders back, head high. Wait to be told where to sit, but if no guidance is forthcoming and you see a chair which you assume is for the interviewer, don't just go and dump yourself onto it. First ask: "May I sit here?" Then sit down.

Incidentally, smoking during the interview, even if the interviewer has offered you a cigarette, is definitely out. Never ask if you may smoke.

Poise and grace: Do not look disturbed or try to avoid the issue when tough questions are put.

Maintain a natural eye-contact with the interviewer and try to control the often unconscious habit of staring aggressively or of looking down. Act and look totally at ease.

Carry all your credentials and certificates with you. Should the interviewer's telephone ring while he is not in the room, do not answer it.

Dress sense: Despite the general casualness, it is a sound practice to show yourself to your best advantage by taking the trouble to look good at a job interview.

Clothes which are good, sober, in which you feel relaxed and at ease and which suit you the best should be chosen for the occasion. Emphasize on depicting yourself as a well-groomed person.

Men: In summer, wear a full-sleeved shirt and tie, opting for a suit in winter.

Ladies: Salwar kameez or saree are both acceptable and can be worn in all climatic conditions. Trousers are out.

In the Interview

Address the interviewers with their usual prefix, while avoiding repetitive use of their names—"Yes, Mr Sharma", "No, Mr Sharma".

Take care to inform yourself about the job and the company before the interview. If being interviewed by SAIL (Steel Authority of India Ltd), find out how many plants they have and where they are located. Prepare convincing answers to such questions as—Why are you interested in working for SAIL?; How do you see your career developing?; and Do you see yourself as an asset to the company and how?

Women who have young children at home may face inquiries about child-care arrangements and their adjusting to the demands of the job.

References/background : Always offer to supply references, giving name address and telephone of each person. Don't forget to get the prior permission of the person whose name you wish to give as a referee.

Redundancy: If you have been made redundant by a previous employer, describe the background to put yourself in the clear. If other members of the staff also suffered similarly, this may be used as supporting evidence.

Sacked: If you were previously sacked for alleged incompetence, you are under no obligation to mention the fact. But if your employer intends to take up references from your previous employer, use suitable explanations such as: misunderstandings about the nature of the job, a personality clash with the boss, being the victim of racist or sexist discrimination, a divorce in the family—these will prepare him in advance.

Do not speak ill of a previous employer in front of a prospective one. You will be earmarked as a disloyal person. Instead, indicate lessons that you have learned.

Rewards and Benefits
Once you are told that you are chosen for the job, you should always raise the topic of salary and conditions of work, if the interviewer seems slow in getting round to the point.

Do not give him the impression that your primary interest lies not in the job itself but in the wages and other benefits it offers, instead just inquire in a general way about these things.

Departure
When the interview is at an end, you should thank the interviewer for his time, shake hands and say good bye, maintaining an optimistic air throughout. It is okay to ask when you are likely to be informed of any decision.

Letter of Confirmation

Remember, at a certain level, the interviewers are looking for someone with whom they can feel comfortable—a face that fits—so be cheerful, optimistic, enthusiastic and confident.

If you are successful, you will receive a letter of confirmation or a contract setting out terms and conditions. These should be very carefully perused before signing, as they often have legal clauses. Always keep a copy of any agreement or contract with you.

ETIQUETTE AT WORK

Give up your seat
The big boss will expect it
an 'I was here first'
Does not mark way
To future promotion
Big or small
The boss certainly does expect it.

*I*n the workplace, people are judged by criteria different from that which prevails outside. Efficiency, power, and success are the main goals. The gentleness that is associated with courtesy may be no match for success here—regrettable as this may sound, but this is the truth.

Most offices have their own way of doing things which can only be learned through observation and experience on the job. However, some general guidelines hold true for all times, like the principles underlying good manners, which do not change with the weather.

Office Code of Behaviour

Every office has its specific code of behaviour that includes the manners the employees exhibit to one another. So watch for a few days, then go along with it.

Too much formality, however, in an office that does not call for it, can make you look stuffy, whereas a lack of good manners towards fellow employees can make you dangerously unpopular. So maintain a balance and learn to survive.

First Name or Formal Style

Addressing staff members by their first names is a commonly

accepted practice, yet the formal style of using prefix and surname as in (Ms Jain) is still practised and can never be considered incorrect. So test the water before taking the plunge.

Much depends on the sector of employment also. Senior members of the office are addressed formally in a respectful way by those who are considerably junior in rank.

Telephone Tactics
The telephone is a double edged weapon—both a boon and a curse. Be polite and brief on the phone. Avoid personal calls as much as possible.

Team Play
Coordination between all the departments is very necessary so that the whole office can work as a team. It not only increases efficiency but inter-personal relationships also.

Handling Rivals
Aggressive and competitive rivalry exists in almost every office. And they can be very treacherous.

How to deal with them? Well, since you have already chosen to run a civilized race, it probably won't do you any good to try to beat such a rival at his own game. The best way out is to beat him at your own best game—good manners and fair play. Any dirty tactics the rival uses can be countered with a little presence of mind and polished manners. It is most likely that in front of his already established ill-reputation, your good manners will shine out and there, you've won the game.

Overcoming Malicious Gossip
Gossip is part of any office's informal channel of communication. The best way is to remain aloof from the gossipers without actually alienating yourself. Earn a reputation for not gossiping and at the same time keep alert to any gossip that may be interesting or helpful to you. Be perceptive so that you can know beforehand, in case some rumour concerning you is going around. Rumours may seem too petty a subject to be bothered about but sadly enough more

than one career has been needlessly destroyed by a competitor spreading malicious gossip. So beware and be prepared.

When a damaging rumour is started, the best way to put an end to it is by confronting its originator as soon as possible and in public. Since you are going to handle this situation in a calm, polite, up-front manner and since there is little doubt about the other person's motives, you have nothing to lose and everything to gain by making the confrontation a public one. A well-mannered public confrontation might go like this:

You: "I heard you told our boss that I was planning to accept a new position with XYZ Corpn."

The gossipmonger (will probably just stutter, too embarrassed and taken aback by this sudden confrontation in public): "Well...".

You: "That's quite a piece of misinformation, isn't it?"

The g. (more stuttering): "I don't know. Is it?"

You: "It certainly is. I've straightened it out with our boss, and I hope you won't be repeating it any more."

End of exchange, end of rumour and no need for any further clarifications. You have already achieved what you wanted.

Helping Out a Colleague

It is considerate to offer help to an overworked colleague but not at the cost of your own work. Offer only when you have free time.

Also, do not earn the reputation of a universal do-gooder. Offer help only when necessary.

Do not brag about the help you have rendered to your colleague, it will give better effect if your colleague himself gives you due credit at an appropriate moment.

Managing Relations with Your Boss

It is very important to be in perfect harmony with your boss. For it is necessary to cater to his ego without going overboard. If your boss is good at his work and highly principled, he will not be particularly interested in having yes-people around. Even if he likes some flattery, do so graciously and within certain limitations. Remember even the largest ego knows when it is being played like a musical instrument.

Discuss your problems about work but never your personal problems. Do not let him see through your weakness. At the same time, do not promise more than what you can deliver.

Handling Subordinates when You have Just Become Boss

This is a tricky situation because till yesterday, you were one among them and today, all of a sudden, you are their senior. Treat them with grace and respect. You are likely to know their natures well. In fact, many of them may even have been your friends till you got promoted. Do not let your newfound authority go to your head and think you must maintain a stiff distance. At the same time, do not treat your friends like favoured people so that they are nicknamed your *chamchas*.

Be friendly, but don't be a pal now. Keep intimate friendships for after-office hours. Intimacy and friendliness are two different things. The former may find yourself in a binding situation which can be harmful to your ambitious career, while the other helps you in achieving further goals.

Handling a Dispute

Sooner or later, you may have a handle a dispute among subordinates. There is an art to doing so. First of all, do not play favourites. Insist that the two fighting employees treat each other with politeness and respect. Then listen to each person's story individually. Be sure to hear both sides. Treat both with the same respect and attention. One good ploy is to ask each person for a written memo detailing the aspects of the dispute. This will give you some breathing room. Also, it will force the arguing persons to confront the issue more directly.

Memos

An ideal office memorandum is short, to the point and civil in tone. Avoid any humorous references, irony or flippant remarks. An office memo should be dated and bear full names of the sender and receiver. A record should be kept of all the distributed memos.

Business Cards

The style of quiet restraint characterizing a visiting card is definitely more assertive in a business card. Business cards should have: the full name, person's designation, name and address of the company, telephone, fax and telex numbers and address in complete.

Office Parties

These are generally staid affairs to meet those in senior positions on informal grounds and encourage a more relaxed approach between the employers and employees.

Circulate: The host should welcome all the guests and then circulate around, saying appropriate things to each person. Punctuality from staff members is essential and they must not stick to one group but circulate.

While juniors must strike up contacts with their seniors, they should be careful not to monopolize an important person throughout the evening.

Women at parties: Even at parties, women must project a business-like image. Avoid taking up unwanted lifts home and enlist the help of your own sex to help you out a sticky situation. If you see a woman colleague trying to fend off unwanted flirtation or advances, be sure to help her out.

Drinks: Alcohol may be freely available but don't imbibe too much. An intoxicated person, be he a junior staff member or a manager, will find it difficult to face his colleagues the next day. An intoxicated male staffer may also incur the wrath of the female members in his organization.

Love in the Office

The working environment affords endless opportunities for romance and marriage, not necessarily in that order. For those unattached people on the lookout for romantic attachments/ affairs, both of which may or may not lead to marriage, the modern office is a common meeting ground.

Rebuffs/Rejecting Advances

A woman may wish to rebuff unwanted attention but may feel constrained to do so, fearing that her job could be jeopardized or her work discriminated against.

How to do this: Responding to unwanted attention requires a cool head, tact and a reliance on good humour. Avoid puncturing a man's vanity, particularly if he is the boss. Instead, put him off by light frivolous conversation or a stern dismissive glance can also convey more than words.

One thing is to be remembered — romance, affairs may develop at the workplace but flaunting a relationship in office must be avoided at all costs.

Men must remember that sexual innuendos and crude remarks (sometimes in reference to a particular woman colleague) must be out of a woman's hearing. It is an insult to your colleague if you do this.

GENERAL HEALTH & BEAUTY CARE

FITNESS

PERFECT HEALTH & AYURVEDA

A Set of 4 Books

DISEASES & COMMON AILMENTS

      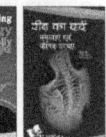

REGIONAL LANGUAGE

(Telugu)　　(Odia)　　(Marathi)　(Bangla)

MISCELLANEOUS

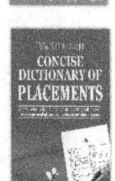

All books available at **www.vspublishers.com**

www.ingramcontent.com/pod-product-compliance
Lightning Source LLC
LaVergne TN
LVHW051158080426
835508LV00021B/2693